CW00494102

Dover
in old picture postcards volume 2

by Bob Hollingsbee

European Library ZALTBOMMEL/THE NETHERLANDS

Cover picture:
Exceptional townscape postcards like this one of the Market Square, postmarked 1911 but probably dating back to the turn of the century, can command high prices. Those illustrating some aspect of social history or depicting a historic event such as an early train crash, car mishap or shipwreck can change hands for £10 to £35 or more. This card by Griggs & Sons, of Dover, who once had printing works in York Street and a stationery shop in Worthington Street, was sent from River to a passenger on the steamship Royal George at Bristol. On the left is Igglesden & Graves' bakery and Dovorian Restaurant which, in recent times, became a book shop but is now tea rooms and a shop again. On the opposite side of the junction with Castle Street are the once extensive furniture showrooms of Flashman & Sons who were well known furnishers and removers in East Kent for many years. Next door are former drapers Killick and Back. The sites of both buildings have been re-developed since the Second World War, while Packham's livery stables on the corner of Castle Street and Church Street, with a useful public clock, has been replaced by the Trustee Savings Bank.

GB ISBN 90 288 6348 6

Introduction

The picture postcard is a product of the twentieth century, and is closely associated with the holiday and tourist business which, hopefully, will revitalise Dover as it faces the 21st century. The Dover district is going all out to attract more of the tourist trade for which there is great potential in East Kent. Postcards published over the years paint a fascinating picture of an era of great change. Dover particularly has seen more changes than in any previous century. It has seen a century of development and decline; of great optimism and of sadness. Industry has developed, then waned, or even failed altogether, but the port of Dover flourished and became the busiest passenger port in the world. Dover now faces the challenge of considerable unemployment and the threat to the ferry trade posed by the opening of the Channel Tunnel.
One of the greatest setbacks and disappointments in recent years was the shock closure of all the Kent coal mines for which the pioneers had such high hopes. Forecasts of a great industrial boom with steel and cement works, and possibly potteries associated with the collieries, following the successful test boring for coal at Dover, proved over-optimistic. This was despite the discovery of not only coal but iron ore and fire clay. Costly problems of incoming water and serious geological faults at times had to be overcome throughout the fifty odd years the pits were in production. Then they were hit by a crippling, year-long strike which was the death-knell of the coalfield already struggling to compete with cheap North Sea gas and oil.
Cheap gas and oil, of course, have been a means of lifting the country out of recession and the twentieth century has also brought about better education and schools, improved living conditions, health and hygiene, and improved care of the elderly. Contrast the care services of today with those of the turn of the century, when a fair number of the local poor, aged and handicapped people, ended their lives in a ward or hospital bed in the workhouse. We also have a fairer penal system and, for a good many there is more leisure time. Sadly, however, high unemployment is still a problem.
The Second World War took its toll on Dover, both in human lives and great material damage due to incessant shelling from German guns on the French coast. Much property was destroyed or damaged beyond repair by bombs, by shells, and flying bombs. Local industry was also affected and lack of finance meant that many of the larger properties damaged could not be renovated; the country was in considerable debt by the end of the war. The appearance of many areas of the town was changed completely by the war, as many interesting old properties, even complete streets, disappeared.
Thankfully many historic buildings survived the war. Others, with a little more vision, might have been saved too. Since the war more interesting properties have followed them into oblivion and the character of some areas has been ruined. Some have fallen victim to re-development, or construction of new roads. This is particularly noticeable in the loss of around a hundred public houses. Many of them were full of character, and some very old, like The Cause is Altered, a landmark at the top of Queen Street. Pulling this down was a tragic mistake. But there was already pressure on the York Street road builders to preserve the much older Roman remains, adjacent to and below the old pub. That at least was done by raising the road level. As early as March 1932 I find a local businessman saying very much the same thing in our local newspaper, the Dover Express, about 'lost' landmarks of the past, which had included the town's attractive Promenade Pier. Writing under the heading 'What Dover might have been' and talking about the town's twelve town gates, the old town wall itself, seven churches, and the old Guildhall standing on wooden pillars in the Market Square,

Edwin Bradley said one could not help but regret 'the lack of vision which permitted the ruthless destruction, or perhaps it would be more truthful to say, the careless indifference' which allowed some of the old landmarks to decay and be demolished as 'useless obstructions'. This same writer went on to pose a question some of those in authority might well ask today: 'Is it possible that we too, like them, do not see the value of our possessions and are letting them slip from our grasp without realising the loss?' We were beginning, he wrote, to value some of our old buildings and monuments, 'but are we yet awake to the beauty of our landscapes, woods and commons?'

A modern parallel lies in the fate of the downland behind the famous Shakespeare Cliff, a landmark not famous enough, it seems, to escape the depredations of the modern planner and road builder. However, there has been a greater awareness of the value of improving access and maintaining amenity areas in the district. The National Trust is doing a grand job with its cliff-top beauty spots and there is improved care and signposting of some public footpaths and bridleways, and protection of wildlife. Sadly, the need to reduce unemployment has seen planning restraints overridden a little too often, in the interests of new development, such as building new homes, superstores or more roads. One major factor contributing to unemployment locally has been a smaller military garrison; at the turn of the century, with a full garrison and soldiers quartered in a number of separate local-barracks, the population peaked at 43,000 of whom at least 3,000 were soldiers. Industrial and other jobs have declined due to increased mechanisation and widespread use of computers. With parts of Dover so devastated by war as far as period buildings are concerned, it is sad to see 'progress' claiming more old properties, such as Christ Church, Coastguard Cottages and nearby 'Sunny Corner' at Aycliffe, the Train Ferry Dock, and all of Last Lane.

On the positive side we once again have the attractive Dickens café, long known as Igglesden and Graves, in the Market Square. The old Metropole building in Cannon Street is restored and the Royal Victoria Hospital building is saved, restored and put to good use, which shows what can be done. There is also a fine seafront and the revitalised White Cliffs Hotel, with the new name of Churchills. Such a pity they had to change the name! We have Castle Street recognised as a conservation area and given a new look, and Snargate Street's remaining properties have a new lease of life. Other plus factors are improved sports facilities, including the Sports Centre and Swimming Pool, and an increasing emphasis on local tourism. This at least has resulted in more recognition and care for some of the town's assets. Dover Castle, a gem of English castles has long been a top tourist attraction and, now managed by English Heritage, is going on to even better things with Napoleonic and Second World War attractions, historic car rallies and other events. We have a fine new Museum with regular high-class exhibitions and Dover's Bronze Age boat is being restored for display. Close by is the White Cliffs Experience which has also brought many visitors to the town, admittedly at considerable cost and controversy. The Old Town Gaol and the unique Grand Shaft triple staircase, up through the cliffs from Snargate Street to the Western Heights, are two more tourist attractions which give a fascinating insight into life in years past.

Among the biggest changes in Dover this century have been the changing emphasis from a naval harbour to a cross-Channel car ferry port, the transfer of the town's shopping centre from the Snargate Street and Market Square areas to Biggin Street, and the impact of the superstores. The almost universal ownership of cars gives most people greatly in-

creased mobility. The coming of television meanwhile has been accompanied by a decline in local cinemas from four to one and there is no theatre now. At the turn of the century the popular daily paper had still to catch on and Dover had three weekly papers publishing local and national news. The telephone service and radio was in its infancy, but there were five deliveries of mail a day, the last at 7 pm! Since those days we have seen a massive growth in holiday passenger traffic, motoring holidays and a boom in freight traffic. And now, with the Channel Tunnel beginning to make a dent in those traffic figures, the town is facing a new challenge with bold plans to bring new business to the Western Docks area, which have already seen a steady stream of cruise liners calling at the port and more leisure sailing craft berthed in the docks.
Dover, through the years, has faced change with optimism and invention, and will continue to do so.

About the Author

Bob Hollingsbee, a Dovorian with more than forty years in local journalism, has been a historical researcher and collector of photographic images of East Kent for thirty years.

Dedication

This book is dedicated to my late father, Eddie Hollingsbee, a fellow journalist, who inspired my interest in local history. And to my wife Kathleen whose encouragement and practical help made possible this and the first volume of 'Dover in Old Picture Postcards.'

1 This picture from a fine water colour painting shows a Dover market scene in 1822. Dominant feature of the Market Square then was the old Guildhall, which was taken down in 1861. Under the Guildhall, in which the Town Council used to meet, were market stalls. The painting, by John Eastes Youden, was presented to the town by former Clerk of the Peace, the late Mr. E.E. Pain. The picture was reproduced as one of a series of forty or more postcards published by the Dover Express newspaper. The Guildhall was built in 1605 and used as a court hall for over 200 years until 1836 when the Dover council bought the Maison Dieu in Biggin Street to convert it into a town hall and court house. The Guildhall was then used as a museum. To the right of the Guildhall is the old Dover gaol which was the scene of an infamous incident in May 1820, when a Folkestone gang wrecked the building and rescued smuggler comrades from their cells. On the other side of the Guildhall is the old Fountain Inn on the corner of King Street, which was then only fifteen ft wide.

2 Dovorians of the past would turn in their graves if they could see what modern planners and road builders have done to the lower slopes of Shakespeare Cliff. Those slopes once gleamed with golden corn or were grassed to provide hay, this no doubt leading to the old name Hay Cliff, and now Aycliffe. Here was one of the tracks used by pack horses plying between coastal towns before the advent of modern transport. This acquired turnpike road status in 1763 but was superseded about twenty years later by the present Folkestone Road. Now the new A20 trunk road carves through a cutting made in the back of the 350ft high Shakespeare Cliff. On the right is part of 'Sunny Corner', once a popular stop for refreshments for walkers along the attractive cliff-top walk. In the distance is a temporary lighthouse which once stood on top of the adjoining Round Down Cliff. This cliff was blown up to help build the railway line to Folkestone 150 years ago. This created a platform on which Dover Colliery was built after the discovery of coal there. Enlarged with spoil from the Channel Tunnel it is now a wildlife haven called Samphire Hoe.

3 This narrow road, leading out of Limekiln Street, with Bulwark Street on the left, is Archcliffe Road, just below Archcliffe Fort. Today the new A20 trunk road from Dover to Folkestone, via Aycliffe and the Alkham Valley, sweeps through the sites of the property shown in the picture. The large building in the centre, towards the right-hand side of the photograph is the former Harbour School, near which years ago was the Archcliffe Brewery. At the top of the hill is the entrance to Archcliffe Fort which escaped demolition when the new road was cut through. In 1934 when the photograph was taken, Archcliffe Road was widened a little prior to the building of much needed council houses off the Old Folkestone Road, which became known as Aycliffe Estate. Quite a number of homes there disappeared, along with the late Ray Pidgeon's Sunny Corner stores, at the foot of the footpath to Shakespeare Cliff and the old Coastguard Cottages, when the new A20 was built.

4 Photographs of the seafront are difficult to date, but this one certainly pre-dates the motor car in Dover. It is from an original 8ins x 6ins glass plate negative of about 1890, when horse-drawn carriages lined up along the promenade, waiting for custom. Today it is visitors' cars which line the railings. Prominent on the left is the Grand Hotel, once one of Dover's larger hotels along with the bigger Burlington Hotel (380 rooms), the top of which peeps over the first of a row of large terraced, four-storey homes fronting the promenade. Both hotels were so badly hit by enemy shelling from the French coast in the Second World War, they were eventually demolished. The owner of the Grand hoped to rebuild, but the council wanted the site in order to re-develop the seafront. The once elegant seafront homes were also damaged, and were demolished some years after the war. One adjacent property that was saved is Marine Court, on the Eastern docks side of the modern Gateway block of flats, which were built on the cleared side of the other houses. The Gateway was built to a design for which there was a national competition because of its important position below Dover Castle.

5 Converted recently into low-cost apartments, in a £2 million plus scheme by the Sanctuary Housing Association, the old Royal Victoria Hospital, pictured on this 1904 postcard, was built as a thanks offering to celebrate the fact Dover had escaped a cholera epidemic, which killed thousands of people in the 1840s. There had been a dispensary for medicines since 1823, and in 1850 it was decided to incorporate this into a hospital. £1,760 was raised by public subscription and it was decided to buy a property known as Brook House, built for paper maker George Dickinson. This was converted into the hospital and it opened in May 1851. At that time it adjoined a cricket ground. Later half an acre of extra land was bought to allow for future hospital growth. Extensions were built with money again raised by a public appeal, as memorials to Queen Victoria and to Sir Richard Dickeson, a wholesale grocer, who was four times mayor. For six years during the last war patients were evacuated to a temporary hospital set up in the old Waldershare Mansion, at the invitation of the Earl of Guilford. Decades after the war most services were transferred to Buckland Hospital in Coombe Valley Road. The 'Vic' received a brief reprieve as a day hospital for the elderly in the late 1960s and then as a stroke unit for a short period.

6 Buckland Hospital which has undergone many changes and survived many threats to its future in recent years, started out as the Dover Union workhouse and hospital. It was built in a then isolated spot near Coombe Farm in the mid 1830s, to replace three older 'poorhouses' at Charlton, River and Martin. Construction was in the style of Bridge workhouse and it was soon enlarged and a hospital was added when the poor of St Mary's Dover poorhouse were also transferred to Buckland in 1836. Further extensions followed, the biggest being the enlargement of the hospital itself for which a loan of £5,800 was raised in 1897. A children's ward and chapel were added and eventually it ceased to be a workhouse. When the old workhouse was built, the area was known as Buckland Bottom, but in 1865 the new road to the hospital became Union Road. It was changed in modern times to reflect its changed image to the more appropriate Coombe Valley Road. An old lane to Coombe Farm itself became St Radigund's Road, leading up the hills to the remains of the old abbey of that name. Near the hospital used to be a brickfield, the products of which were used to build many local homes.

7 The old Castle Hill tollgate, pictured about 120 years ago, stood on the ridge of the hill a little above the present turning to Deal, the road to which used to be a toll road. The old turnpike road turned rather sharply off the Guston Road just beyond the brow of the hill. Through the gate, removed about 1878, was Prescott's Pond, on the site of which the old sergeants' mess at Connaught Barracks was built. The name above the toll house door is Thomas Munn. The board above his name carries a large public notice, which no doubt gave details of tolls charged to horse-drawn and other traffic. One of the last tenants of the house was 'Cock' Linnet. John Linnet was a shepherd who cared for sheep grazing on the surrounding slopes. Later he was a night watchman for the Council. The Prescotts farmed in the area for centuries and one of them was responsible for the conversion of Captain Samuel Taverner, who had been appointed captain of Deal Castle by Cromwell. Captain Taverner went on to become pastor of the Dover Baptist community.

8 Kearsney Abbey is the name given to one of Dover's most attractive parks and also to this impressive building which once stood there. The parkland forms a pedestrian link between Lewisham Road, River and the Alkham Valley Road and is one of the jewels of Dover. The 'abbey' was in fact built in 1822 by Dover banker J.M. Fector for his family, using stone from the old Dover town walls. It featured a fine wood panelled library and billiard room which, sadly, is the only part left, now serving as a café and shop. The main building had to be demolished because of dry rot, some time after the old Dover Town Council acquired the parkland property. Mr. Fector was a principal of the Minet & Fector Bank, taken over in 1842 by the National and Provincial, now part of the NatWest Bank. At one time he lived at Kearsney Manor, now a nursing home, across the road from the Abbey. He also built Laureston House, at Laureston Place, off Castle Hill, the property being named after his wife, who was Miss Laurie.

9 Old Cannon Street, typical of Dover's narrow main thoroughfare before widening, just prior to the turn of the century. The date is 1893, just before the shop premises with a colonnade, on the left, between St Mary's Church and the Market Square, were demolished. St Mary's is one of the three Dover churches mentioned in the Domesday Book and its tower dates from the Norman period. Claims that there are remains of Saxon church foundations are disputed, but early this century part of a Roman bathhouse was found under the floor of the church, on the Market Square side. Note the old Royal Oak Inn on the right, now gone. A Captain Cannon was Deputy Governor of Dover Castle in the Commonwealth period. John Cannon, his son, mayor in 1716, was a property owner in Cannon Street, being a baker and farmer. He had a farmyard on the west side and bakery on the east. Another descendant was a Baptist minister in the town.

10 This aerial view of Dover, with Cannon Street on the right, leading into the Market Square, dates from 1924 and is remarkable for showing the number of properties which used to stand between St Mary's Church in the centre foreground and the sea at the top of the picture. It is one of a series of Aerofilms Ltd photographs reproduced in the Dover Express newspaper over a period of about ten years from around 1923. Some of these were reproduced as postcards by Dawsons of Dover. Among many prominent features are Flashman's former showrooms, extending from the Market Square up Castle Street and behind other property, to the old Phoenix Brewery. Owned for many years by the Leney family this brewery dated back to at least 1740. Today the busy new A20 to the Eastern Docks cuts across the top half of the area shown in the picture.

11 A busy but relatively tranquil time in the Market Square in the days midway between the two world wars, when the old Dover Corporation Tramway service was still running, and when a woman and child could stand nonchalantly in the middle of the road, waiting for the next tramcar. The postcard view, with only a hint of a bus terminus to the left, is in marked contrast to the busy scene at the same spot after the Second World War when there was a roundabout in the centre of the Square and a constant stream of traffic. Today it is tranquil once more, most of the Square having been turned into a pedestrian precinct with a fountain and flowers. Cannon Street, leading out of it in the centre, has also been pedestrianised. Left is a grocer's horse-drawn van making a delivery and behind it is one of the early single-decker buses, with solid tyres and gun carriage style wheels, bearing a Hythe destination board. It was a forerunner of the East Kent Road Car Company's fleet. Behind the bus is the old Carlton Club, now demolished, former headquarters of the Conservative Association. Coming out of Cannon Street is a heavy steam traction engine hauling a large trailer resembling an old threshing machine.

12 The highly popular Royal Hippodrome Theatre. Built as the Tivoli Theatre on the site of an earlier theatre established in 1790, it became the Hippodrome in the early part of this century. Its manager could proudly boast that the show went on, to entertain both civilians and thousands of servicemen and women, despite bombing and shelling throughout the Second World War. Actors, comedians and even strippers helped maintain morale until one of the last shells fired by enemy guns on the French coast brought the curtain down for good, about midday on September 25th, 1944. The 600-seat theatre had its entrance and bars in Snargate Street while the rear backed onto Northampton Street which ran parallel with the Wellington Dock. The manager was Mr. H.R. Armstrong, and his assistant from 1942 Dick Whittamore. Stars appearing included Tommy Trinder, Beryl Reid, Evelyn Laye and Tessie O'Shea. Demolition finally 'brought down the house' in January 1951, the massive walls being toppled using the steel cables of a winch looped through the windows.

13 This interesting old postcard picture taken between two world wars is of Cannon Street and depicts the former Metropole Hotel (opened in 1896) and restaurant with the Metropole grocery store, reminiscent of Internationals which were a prominent feature of most towns, and, on the right Alstons ladies' and gents' tailors which were still in business until recent times. Interesting is the combination on the left of Timothy Whites the chemist's, and MacDonald & Co Ltd.'s 'guaranteed teeth' advertised in the windows over this shop. This imposing four-storey block was built on the site of the historic Royal Oak public house. Behind the once ornate hotel entrance was later established one of the town's four major cinemas, the Plaza, later to become a bingo hall. Standing opposite St Mary's Church the whole block is a present day 'success story'. Threatened with demolition, having fallen into disrepair, it has now been completely restored and a number of interesting shops have opened on the ground floor, but there is no hotel.

14 Dover High Street when it was lined by comparatively small shops on either side, all providing a living for their owners. Traffic was two-way and the odd horse and cart was still a familiar sight making deliveries. The year is 1953, Coronation year of Queen Elizabeth II. The photograph was evidently taken from an upper window of the Eagle public house at the corner of Tower Hamlets Road and London Road. Bottom right is an old shoe shop which in recent times became a video shop. Many of the shops and a sprinkling of homes on the left have disappeared to make way for the building of the Charlton Shopping Centre and the former Sainsbury supermarket. In the distance are the towers of the Town Hall, or Maison Dieu, on the left and, opposite, the United Reformed Church, originally the Congregational Church. The Coronation was marked in a special way by the local paper, the Dover Express, which featured news on its front page where there were normally only classified advertisements, and in particular births, marriages and deaths, until the early 1960s. Local celebrations lasted three weeks.

15 Old Park Mansion, believed to be part of the old Manor of Archers Court, near Whitfield, was at one time the home of Major Robert Lawes JP who partly rebuilt it in 1870. But for many years until recently Old Park has been the site of the barracks of the now departed Junior Leaders' Regiment of the Royal Engineers. Since they left the site has been used for light industry, with some of the old married quarter homes still used by the Army. Old Park was once known as Little Archers Court, and the estate eventually became the home of the Honeywood family, one of whom, Colonel Henry Honeywood, served under rebel Oliver Cromwell. Major Lawes, who died in 1907, sold a plot of land to Dover Council, which enabled Barton Road to be opened up to join with London Road at Buckland Bridge. His son, Robert Murray Lawes, caused a bit of a stir in Dover by becoming the first local man to own a motor car, a 1897 4hp open Daimler, which regularly takes part in the annual London to Brighton veteran car run.

16 Public clocks were in much greater demand in years gone by when the average working man was expected to work up to six and a half days per week, including Saturday mornings. This picture shows a clock on the corner of Cherry Tree Avenue and London Road, at Martin's the stationer, newsagent, confectioner and tobacconist. Next door on the right is the Little Covent Garden greengrocer's shop. Around the corner, in Cherry Tree Avenue were the Connaught Coach Works and there were mills and a gas works nearby, providing employment for many manual workers. Eighty years on, there is still a newsagent's shop on the corner.

17 This fine postcard of around 1900-1910 gives a good impression of the size of the old Burlington Hotel on the right of the picture, with large frontages to Woolcomber Street and Liverpool Street, now part of Townwall Street. Later converted into apartments it was demolished after Second World War damage. In front of it was Clarence Lawn across which there was a view to the harbour over the old Promenade Pier, the shore end of which can be seen on the left. The large built-up area in the foreground and the adjoining churchyard of Old St James' Church, which is off the picture to the right, were cleared after the war and the Dover Sports Centre built on the site. At the end of Marine Parade is the once attractive Prince of Wales Pier, the striking, latticed metal work of which, sadly, had to be filled in to give shelter to the Hovercraft terminal when that was built. Practically every building in the foreground has now disappeared, thanks largely to war damage, subsequent neglect or lack of money for investment.

18 Commercial Quay, facing the Wellington Dock, now a yacht marina, was once little more than a track for pedestrians alongside the smelly old pent, which was hemmed in on the landward side by the backyards and outbuildings of properties in Snargate Street. Prominent on the left in this picture, taken soon after the First World War is Sharp & Enright's, ship chandlers and sail makers, which has been at the port five generations spanning nearly 150 years. When Commercial Quay properties were cleared for dock development before the last war the firm simply moved one street back to almost identical premises in Snargate Street, and is still there. Standing in the doorway on the left is believed to be one-time owner Sidney Sharp. For neighbours the shop had a profusion of public houses, including the Mariners' Arms, Old and New Commercial Quay Inns, Grand Shaft Inn, Standard Inn, London Packet Inn, Lord Wolseley, Wellesley Inn, Golden Anchor Hotel and Union Hotel! Now the new A20 runs over the sites.

19 This interesting view is across the Wellington Dock with an old Harbour Board paddle steamer tug in the foreground and the former Sailors' Bethel Home on the corner of Northampton Street where the road used to curve round into Snargate Street. It is an illustration of a battle which rages even today between developers and town planners trying to set and maintain standards. The huge Quaker Oats sign put up on the famous White Cliffs of Dover behind what is now the Masonic Hall, created an uproar. It led to letters being published in The Times and other national newspapers. The Society for the Prevention of Abuses of Advertising organised a petition to get the sign removed. A clever Dover Town Council included a clause in a bill it was promoting in Parliament governing tramway routes, to outlaw this and other un-licensed sites. That was in 1901, making Dover Council one of the first in the U.K. to have powers to control advertising.

20 The Royal Ship Hotel which once extended into two large buildings on historic Customs House Quay at the Granville Dock, was once one of the most important hotels in the town. It had many distinguished guests through the first half of the 19th century. They would often need time to recover after an uncomfortable crossing of the Channel in small steamers, before continuing their journey to the capital or elsewhere. Their every comfort was looked after by several important families in succession, the Wrights, Birminghams and Worthingtons, who used to own or manage the hotel. The site of the buildings was later occupied by Bradley's corn stores and in more recent times by the warehouses of Hammonds, shipping agents at the port for about a century. On top of the cliffs on the right of the picture are military barracks which had a unique triple staircase access, known as the Grand Shaft, down through the cliff to Snargate Street below. The staircase is now a tourist attraction, but the barrack buildings were demolished some years after the Second World War. The photograph was taken by Snargate Street photographer Mr. G.T. Amos who earned some degree of fame for recording a long series of sailing ships calling at the port.

21 Lord Warden Hotel, a prominent landmark in the Western Docks area since its opening in 1853, survives as offices. Known as Southern House, it was for years, until recent times, the British Rail headquarters at the port. Hopefully destined to be preserved, the building has many historic links with the past and many secrets could be revealed, as they say, if the walls could talk. Here stayed many a monarch heading to or from the Continent in the days of the steam packet. Charles Dickens was a regular guest and became a friend of Mr. and Mrs. John Birmingham who ran the hotel in the early days. Mr. Birmingham was four times mayor of Dover and among his guests was Napoleon III and his wife Eugenie. Later Louis Bleriot was a guest. The hotel had 110 bedrooms. The somewhat austere building of today was once one of the night spots of the town, for between the wars there was much entertaining and dancing in the fine ballroom, and its ornamental ceilings and basement kitchens were a sight to behold. During the Second World War it had a different role. It became a rest centre for troops on leave from France and was then taken over by the Royal Navy. Post-war hopes of renovation were dashed when the railway took it over as offices. Later still, part of it became a Customs and Excise headquarters.

Above: A 1920s postcard view of Dover's Marine Station, as the former Western Docks Station was called for most of its life. Now transformed into the town's new Liner Terminal for cruise ships of all kinds it is another of Dover's modern success stories. It seems a shame, however, that famous trains, like the now defunct Golden Arrow or Night Express, can no longer pull into it. A railway link-up for liner traffic was made along the Prince of Wales' Pier as long ago as 1905 but a few years later work began on widening the Admiralty Pier to build the Marine Station.

Beneath: Battle of Britain Class engine 601 Squadron hauls a Golden Arrow boat express, with Pullman coaches out of the Marine Station, seen on the right, towards the Shakespeare Cliff tunnel on the Charing Cross line. The date is the late 1950s or early 1960s. It was fitting that a surviving engine of this class, the 'Iron Duke' (he was the Duke of Wellington after whom the Lord Warden Hotel was named) should haul the last train to use the station, carrying 400 steam enthusiasts, in 1994.

23 This interesting picture was published by A.H. Pointer at his Royal Bazaar, Snargate Street, before the turn of the century as a trade card. It depicts the remarkable catamaran steamer Calais-Douvres built to shield passengers from the dreaded mal-de-mer which made countless travellers ill in the choppy Dover Strait. Not so impressive in appearance as an earlier catamaran, the Castalia, the Calais-Douvres was faster, and popular for a while, carrying 1,080 passengers. But the idea didn't really work, the 1,924 ton ship with engines of 4,600hp and capable of 14½ knots, was costly to run and not properly tested in winter conditions. But it was in service for about nine years from 1878 to 1887 and is believed to have ended up as a coal storage hulk. An even more unusual vessel designed to eleminate the effect of swell was the Bessemer, with two pairs of paddle wheels and a floating saloon. The saloon was never put to the test because the vessel itself was too difficult to steer and she was scrapped after colliding with a pier in Calais.

24 Above: This fine view along the Admiralty Pier towards the Lord Warden Hotel (later called Southern House) is believed to date from around 1899. The original print is from a 12" x 10" glass plate negative and shows work just beginning, on the right, on the Prince of Wales' Pier, which was completed in January 1902. On the left is a fine example of a Stirling Mail engine, possibly built at Ashford, with original 'muzzle loader' funnel. It is hauling a mail van and two carriages with a similar train behind it. The nearest steamer is believed to be the Marie Henriette, with the Clementine behind. On the skyline between the funnels is the old garrison church, now demolished, on the Western Heights. Above Snargate Street to the right are the Grand Shaft Barracks and, on the opposite side, the Citadel barracks and South Front military hospital, all later demolished.

Beneath: This handsome, cross-Channel passenger steamer was the first of a new breed of fast vessels which entered service in 1903. The much loved Queen, pictured alongside the Admiralty Pier with a double headed boat train waiting, was to earn fame during the First World War, rescuing 2,000 refugees from a French vessel sunk by a German submarine in 1914. Sadly, however, two years later to the day, she was herself sunk by enemy destroyer, but only after all those on board had left the ship.

25 A fine view of the Wellington Dock about 1899, with the successful paddle-steamer Calais-Douvres II, not to be confused with the twin-hulled cross-channel steamer of the same name. In the foreground is the schooner Erme squeezed alongside. The Calais-Douvres made her inaugural crossing on 31st May 1889, and was in service in the Channel for eleven years before leaving Dover about 1900 to begin another successful spell of service operated by the Isle of Man Steam Packet Company under her new name Mona. She was capable of twenty knots and is believed to have been the first cross-channel ferry lit throughout by electricity. Her bow shows clearly the London Chatham and Dover Railway Company crest. The older and much smaller paddler, the Calais, in service from 1896 to 1916 is alongside. Later re-named Au Revoir, she was sunk by a U-Boat in 1916. The Grand Shaft Barracks are clearly shown on the cliff top, and squeezed among the quayside public houses to the right is the sailmaker sign of ships' chandlers Sharp and Enright featured on another page.

26 The Home Secretary, the French Ambassador, British and French railway officials and the Lord Warden of the Cinque Ports were among VIPs at the opening of Dover Train Ferry Dock on October 12th, 1936. The Hampton Ferry, one of a three-strong fleet of specially designed train ferries, was dressed overall with flags and bunting for the occasion. The initial crossing with many distinguished guests on board was to Calais, but Dunkirk was the 'twin' port selected by the Southern Railway. Two days later the Night Ferry service began, a special train leaving Victoria Station at 10pm and arriving in Paris at 8.55 the following day. The crossing to Dunkirk took about three hours and forty minutes. There were two crossings a day with passenger trains and a day time service with freight wagons in between. Sleeping car passengers boarded trains at Victoria and remained in their berths until they arrived in Paris. 25 cars could also be carried. Work began on building the train ferry dock in 1933. The Channel Tunnel has made train ferries and the old dock superfluous.

27 The Twickenham Ferry, fresh from the shipyard where it was built, negotiates the tidal harbour with the help of port tug Lady Duncannon. The ferry was one of three sister ships launched in 1934 which were ready before the train ferry dock had been completed. Two of them were laid up for some time in the Wellington Dock alongside Commercial Quay waiting to enter service. Train ferries were first run for military purposes from Richborough in the First World War and were a great success. Much later a peace-time service began between Harwich and Zeebrugge, and in 1931 to Calais, but Dunkirk was Southern Railway's ultimate choice. The original Dover train ferries were each 364ft long, with a speed of fifteen knots. They ended their operations from Dover in 1972 when the Hampton Ferry was towed away for scrap. She was replaced by the freight carrier Anderida. From 1980 only railway wagons were carried.

28 The largest Atlantic liners once called at Dover, including the Amerika, pictured on the day of its first visit in 1905, when it berthed at the Prince of Wales' Pier. This prestige traffic was the result of the initiative of two of Dover's distinguished citizens, Sir William Crundall, who was mayor thirteen times and chairman of Dover Harbour Board, and Mr. Worsfold Mowll, Register of the Board. Both are pictured on another page. Sadly, work on completing the massive Admiralty harbour at Dover hampered the berthing of the big ships and the port soon lost this valued traffic after the liner Deutschland was damaged entering port in 1906. It was so seriously damaged in a collision with the Prince of Wales' Pier, it had to cancel its voyage to New York. Another liner, Prinz Joachim, also hit the Breakwater. Thanks to the efforts of Dover shipping agents George Hammond & Co. there was a brief revival in the 1930s. After the Second World War there were occasional visits by smaller cruise vessels. A new purpose-built Dover Cruise Liner Terminal was opened in 1996 at the former Dover Marine railway station at the Admiralty Pier.

29 Decked with flags and bunting two of the heaviest steam locomotives on the South Eastern and Chatham Railway, weighing 180 tons, with the Mayor, Sir William Crundall, deputy chairman of Dover Harbour Board, on the footplate, cross the new Wellington Dock swing bridge at Union Street, in June 1904. The ceremony marked the opening of a new railway link to a berth for trans-Atlantic liners at the end of the Prince of Wales Pier. Two locomotives were used to prove the safety of the bridge and test the railway link created from the old Harbour Station along Strond Street. This link was completed by track laid along the pier to a station built at the liner berth. Those who joined the train for the crossing of the seafront, involving a gradient of 1 in 30, and the trip along the pier, included Dover lawyer Mr. E. Worsfold Mowll, Register of Dover Harbour Board, who is pictured with Sir William on another page. It was hoped that later a viaduct would be built to make a direct rail link with the Town Station, next to the Lord Warden Hotel, but it was never built.

30 A Dover life-saving crew made up of local seamen in 1912. Four of them, Claw, Burville, Prescott and Pilcher, were posing for the picture with their colleagues, after being presented with Board of Trade medals for 25 years' service. The picture was taken at the town end of East Cliff at, what for years has been a 'parking lot' for military owned sailing craft. The life-saving apparatus crew, as they were known, are pictured with the carriage containing rocket launching apparatus for firing rescue lines to ships in distress, breeches buoy equipment and lamps. Pictured, left to right are: The Mayor William Bromley, a Board of Trade Inspector (name unknown), William Gibbons, Benjamin Burville, William Bingham, Andrew Claw, William George Burville, Benjamin Pilcher, John (Jack) Burville, Harry Bingham, Tarling Spain, Jack Bingham and a Coastguard Officer (name unknown). William and Benjamin Burville lived at East Cliff and parts of their homes were in the Cliff caves.

31 Now reclaimed from the sea for modern harbour traffic this is a view of the Camber, in the Eastern Docks, pictured in 1919-1920 when the submarine pens area was a graveyard of once proud warships. In war time it was a base for fast motor torpedo boats and gunboats but afterwards condemned warships were moored there awaiting attention from Stanlee's nearby ship breakers' yard. Those warships included HMS St Vincent, Superb, Vengeance, Inflexible and Canopus. On the right, at berths in the outer harbour, are some old destroyers which may be awaiting a similar fate. Further out in the harbour is the black oval shape of the upturned hull of the gun monitor Glatton which, loaded with ammunition, caught fire and posed a major threat to port and town. The Royal Navy responded by evacuating the survivors of the blaze and sinking the ship with torpedoes. Bodies of men who died in the fire were not recovered until many years later when the vessel was lifted and brought ashore to be broken up alongside the West Jetty.

32 The Dover or Shakespeare Colliery at the top of the seashore west of Shakespeare Cliff in the early 1900s. Geologists speculated there was coal in Kent back in the 1850s but it took the abandonment of an exploratory Channel Tunnel to bring about a serious search for coal. The Board of Trade backed by the Army halted the tunnel when it had been bored 6,300ft out to sea. Rail chief Sir Edward Watkin, of the Channel Tunnel Company, then decided to bore for coal. In February 1890 rail engineer Francis Brady struck coal in 14 seams, the best, of four feet thick at 2,274 ft. Iron ore and fire clay suitable for potteries was also found and a boom for East Kent predicted. Steelworks, collieries, cement works and potteries were expected to follow. But from the start there was massive flooding and, when the first shaft reached 300ft, water gushed in drowning eight sinkers. Work went on, ownership changed hands, new ideas were tried but eventually, in 1915, the pit was abandoned. More easily worked seams were worked at Tilmanstone and Snowdown. The main railway line between Dover and Folkestone is on the right.

33 A low level aerial view of the old gas works in Coombe Valley Road in 1950, before the plant was greatly enlarged and modernised. Near the gas holder in the foreground is the Primrose, formerly Primrose Hall public house. The main Dover to Canterbury railway line runs across the picture towards the centre. The main street, London Road, is near the top showing Mannering's Mill and the former Palmer's coach builders workshops, the site of which is now Kingsford Court flats, top right. The gas works was enlarged several times, eventually producing gas from coal for towns from Ashford to Canterbury and Thanet. Improvements in 1950 saw it replace plants at Deal, Folkestone and New Romney. In 1906 the Dover Gas Company chairman was Willsher Mannering. The town's first gas works was at the seaward end of Trevanion Street, a site now occupied by Dover sports centre. The gas works was sufficiently advanced to illuminate the centre of Dover in 1823. There have been works in Coombe Valley Road since 1864. Today the few remaining gas holders in East Kent provide storage for North Sea gas.

34 One 'victim' of the many changes which have hit Dover in the past century, is the town's one surviving newspaper, the Dover Express, established in 1858 by John Thomas Friend. A new road plan, which saw narrow York Street widened to a dual carriageway to carry heavy traffic from Folkestone Road to the Eastern Docks, required that the old Snargate Street printing works be demolished. It also forced a merger with the F.J. Parsons group of newspapers and the transfer of printing away from the town for the first time in 110 years. The picture was taken during a serious fire which nearly destroyed those printing works and offices, in May 1962. Staff formed a human chain to save valuable records and hundreds of bound copies of back issues of the Dover Express, and other papers going back to the 1790s. While based in Snargate Street, four generations of the Bavington Jones family owned and ran the paper. The paper's offices later moved to 22 Castle Street and, later, to the present site in High Street.

35 This photograph shows Chitty's old corn mill at Charlton Green, part of which survived until recent years, with the Red Lion public house on the right-hand side of the picture. The photograph dates from the early years of this century. The site of the mill is now occupied by Halfords store and car park. The mill was a prominent target for German gunners in the Second World War, and was too badly damaged to be repaired after the war. The Charlton Green Mill was once the centre of a big trade, the owners, the Chitty family, being quick to adopt modern roller milling methods, power being provided by the once fast-flowing river Dour. Mr. G.W. Chitty built up his business with windmills at Deal and later took over the oil crushing and flour mills of William Kingsford on the Charlton Green site. Mill output was widely distributed in the UK and exported.

36 Marine store dealer Jim Todd books-in a load of rags and scrap iron at his yard in Magdala Road; the year is 1910. The business of E. Todd also occupied premises at one time at 77 Folkestone Road. Also in the original picture, given to former ambulance officer and a local historian Joe Harman, of St Radigund's Road, Dover, by Jim's son Len Todd, are Tommy House, 'Pearly' Bill and Jack Tyler. The building in the background backed onto the embankment of the Dover to Canterbury railway line. The property was close to the former Alfred Kingsford Windmill Brewery and an adjoining brickfield, the bricks from which were no doubt used to build many of the surrounding homes. The brewery and windmill, used to raise water from a well for use in brewing, have been demolished and the site is now occupied by Kingsford Court, a block of sheltered homes.

37 This charming family photograph of 1904 was taken in London Road, Dover, on what used to be the main A2 road to London at the junction with Whitfield Hill. The bend on the left of the picture is now considerably altered, the bank on the right having been cut away to improve visibility. The land beyond the wall was part of the Old Park estate of Major Murray Lawes of Whitfield. Pictured with the horse and trap are members of the Goldsack family of Coldred Court Farm, Coldred, Charlotte Goldsack, Rosetta 'Fanny' Dashwood (née Goldsack), Flora Goldsack and Rosetta's children. The year after the picture was taken Flora married John Fisher of Faversham and later had three children, including Mrs. Gwen Bates of Astley Avenue, Dover, who lent me the original photograph.

38 For thirty years Dover had its own car factory which produced car bodies for Peugeot, in the early days, for Armstrong Siddeley and Rolls-Royce. For a few years it also made coach bodies for the East Kent Road Car Company. The hand-built cars, on manufacturers' chassis, were produced by coachworks established by George Sacre Palmer in about 1770. The firm, which began in Priory Street, took over the Kingsford Brewery premises on the corner of London Road and Coombe Valley Road and ran the Connaught Coachworks in nearby Cherry Tree Avenue. This photograph dates from about 1908 when Walter J. Palmer of River, son of George, was the boss and the firm had an order for fifty cars with Peugeot chassis and engines. In their hurry to stage this picture they forgot to put a tyre on one wheel! For a time the business was run as Connaught Coach Works and Palmers Ltd. But the name G.S. Palmer on the arched sign survived into recent times. Rolls-Royce cars, in a variety of styles, were built in Cherry Tree Avenue workshops. Palmers closed down just before the Second World War as contracts petered out due to mass production methods. Two leading craftsmen started the vehicle repair firm of Jenkins & Pain, in the same building. Kingsford Court now occupies the site.

39 In 1978 a Dover road haulage business which had begun with horse-drawn carts and buses celebrated its centenary. P.W. Sneller Ltd. was a family business with origins going back to the opening of a butcher's shop in De Burgh Street, off Tower Hamlets Road, Dover, in 1867. Progress of the firm was punctuated with events that bring the past vividly to life, like the day the company was asked to transport Bleriot's frail monoplane from Northfall Meadow, where it landed in 1909, to the railway station, en route to an exhibition in London. Sadly a general rundown in the economy forced the Cherry Tree Avenue firm, headed by Harold Sneller of Crabble Hill, Dover, to close down at the end of 1979. For years the firm's horse-bus ran between Buckland and the local railway stations. Harold's father, Percy, was at the head of the firm until he became a victim of a German raid on the town in 1942. At its peak the firm had about seventeen modern lorries, vehicles having progressed from one horse power wagons to 150 hp giants.

40 This fine charabanc picture dates from about 1920 and was given to me by former Jenkins & Pain coachworks boss at Dover, Mr. Bert Pain of Whitfield, who was born in 1900. A tall square-section chimney stack in the background at the former Kingsford Windmill Brewery, in London Road, helps pinpoint the spot as Cherry Tree Avenue. The charabancs of 'Father' Eric Wills, of Cheriton, are standing opposite some of the workshops of coachbuilders George Sacre Palmer, whose company's main works were at the old Kingsford brewery site. At least two of the men in the picture were Palmer's workers. George Rye is standing in front of the second, Dennis coach, and Jack Fenn is the man with a flat cap seated next to the driver of the fourth, AEC coach. At least three of the coaches have solid tyres and heavy gun carriage type wheels, and the registration numbers all date from 1917-1920. The old cottage behind the charabancs stood near the corner of London Road. For many years now the site has been a tyre fitter's depot.

Above: This charabanc with removable top and open sides is a Leyland, registration number D8200, which operated a service between Dover and St Margaret's Bay. In the background is the corner of William Eastes' animal feed store. According to the 1906 directory he was also a farmer. Next door is family grocer Percy Ransom's shop and hidden by the charabanc is the cycle shop of J. Austen. Just off the picture to the right was the Imperial Dairy shop of A. Woodhams, who sold milk and greengrocery from farms at Capel, Hougham and Chilverton Elms at the end of Elms Vale Road.

Beneath: In 1910 people would stop and stare when a car or lorry appeared in the street, especially one like this striking chauffeur-driven model, a French Brasier. The car, with heavy gun carriage style wheels and early pneumatic tyres, is pictured outside the Albion Hotel, in East Cliff. The chauffeur was Robert Clarke, who worked for Lady Elizabeth Vaughan and her husband. Robert went on to drive in the Army Service Corps in the First World War, both in France and Salonica, and his compassion for a fellow man got him into a spot of trouble. That was because he refused to shoot one of the enemy, a boy of 17. After the war Robert worked at Chitty's Mill in Dover.

42 Some of Dunlop's earliest pneumatic tyres are shown on this splendid French Brasier car of one-time Dover doctor and surgeon Mr. J.L. Rubel of The Red House, now Redlands, at London Road, near the top of Crabble Hill. The doctor employed a chauffeur, Charlie Butcher, who may have posed this 1905 picture in the road near the house, with the doctor's two daughters, Georgina and Margaret, at the wheel. The road widens at this point and it was a favourite spot for photographers to set up pictures of charabanc outing groups, many of which were reproduced as postcards. Mr. Rubel was in practice in Dover as a physician and surgeon with a Mr. Robins. The chauffeur, from River, was also a driver for Mr. Murray Lawes, who lived at Old Park Mansion, Whitfield. Mr. Lawes owned what was reputedly Dover's first locally owned car, an open 1897 Daimler, which still exists. The photograph was lent to me by Mrs. Gwen Bates, of Astley Avenue, Dover.

43 Above: Pictured soon after its arrival at Dover is the ill-fated tram car which was involved in a tragic accident in Crabble Road in 1917, referred to in my first book on old Dover postcards. The incident has a place in history, as it was for many years the worst traffic accident involving a public service vehicle. The postcard pictured is from the collection of former Dover Corporation Tramways conductor Mr. Joe Harman. Tram car No. 20 is pictured at the River terminus around 1906-7, with Mr. Harman's father, Percy, the conductor standing beside it. The line to River had not long been open when the photograph was taken and there were then only a few houses built along Lewisham Road.

Beneath: In the First World War when thousands of local men were away fighting for their country in the services, women took on a variety of new roles. Some, like diminutive May Archer, seen on the platform of this Dover tramcar No 23, became a familiar sight working as conductresses on the Corporation tram service. This is a copy of a picture she dropped in to the Dover Express office to prove it when she was 90, in 1985. In the background is Buckland Avenue. Another trailblazer was Elizabeth 'Biddy' Kay who became a driver of an open-top tramcar like this one. Her younger sister Lillian Kay will be known to many as a former headmistress of the Dover Girls' Grammar School.

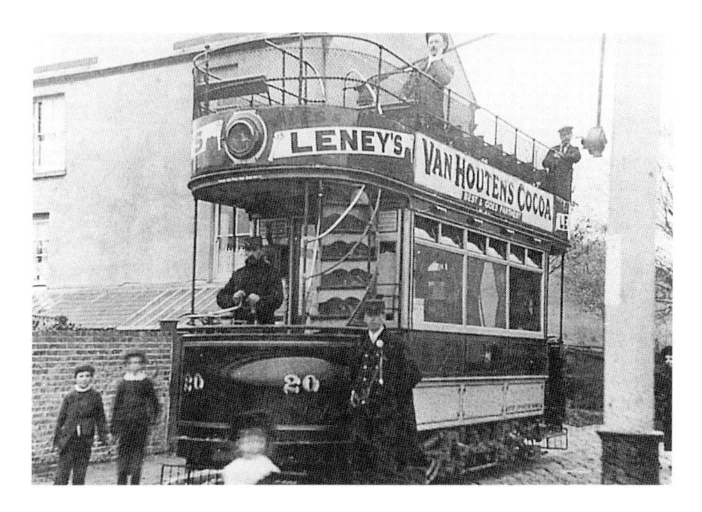

44 When a gas explosion damaged the road and halted the Dover Corporation tramway service along Snargate Street in December 1925, the Town Council hit upon the idea of a 'minibus' service. Few will remember it, however, because it only lasted fourteen days! The only vehicle they seemed able to find was this Model T Ford charabanc alleged to have seating for eighteen, which was hired at £2 a day. Council staff acted as drivers. The bus ran from the old Bethel Corner, at the corner of Snargate Street and Northampton Street to the tram terminus at the Crosswall pier, Granville Dock. The charabanc is pictured outside the Hotel de Paris, now demolished, near the pier. Incidentally the cost of petrol for the two weeks was £41 and there was an estimated saving on electricity of about £10. The average number of passengers carried was only seven. The photograph is believed to have been taken by tramways staff man George Archer, who lived at Alkham.

45 The mayor of the time, Henry Minter Baker, a wholesale grocer and farmer, is reported to have taken the controls on Dover's first official tramcar run from Buckland tramshed to the Pier. That was in September 1897. In this picture above, on a sadder occasion, the closure of the tramway on the last day of December 1936, it was again the serving mayor, Alderman H. Madgett Norman, at the controls. He is third from the left in the back row with his wife beside him. Next to her, extreme right, is the official driver, Percy Sutton, while conductor H. Blaskett is on the extreme left of the footplate. Fifth from the right in the front row is Tramways inspector Fred Pay who drove the first Maxton cars 39 years before. After this final passenger run, from Worthington Street to Maxton, those returning to the town centre took a ride on the first town service East Kent bus, a 53 seater driven by W.F. Fairweather with A. Corteel as conductor. The photograph was by Farringdon & Harrison of Castle Studio, Maison Dieu Road, Dover. It is a matter of deep regret that the last tramcar was not preserved. Most were destroyed by burning.

46 The Crossley ambulance of the Dover division of the St John Ambulance Brigade in February 1924, apparently pictured outside the now demolised St Bartholomew's Church, which was on the corner of London Road and Templar Street. The local brigade was established about 1898 and behind the spare wheel is the name of the then secretary H.R. Geddes, who is the man with a trilby hat standing behind the bonnet of the engine. On the left of the picture is Sergeant G. Gore, described as transport officer in local directories of the time, and next to him Private Hammond. In front of the engine is Mr. Tupper. Who the driver is I don't know, but he is certainly well prepared for some rough weather, with cap, ear flaps and high collar, the side of the cab having only canvas sheeting to keep out the rain and cold.

47 This picture, believed to date from 1925, is of the dignitaries and officials of the Cinque Ports on the occasion of a meeting in Dover of the Court of Brotherhood & Guestling, attended by the Lord Warden Earl Beauchamp. I include it because it depicts a notorious bottleneck in Biggin Street and some interesting old properties. In 1963 these were demolished to widen the road. The little shops adjoining the Public Library were pulled down and new premises, with little character, built in their place. Among the properties lost was the Salutation Inn which had provided rest and refreshment for workmen and travellers between Dover and Canterbury for 300 years. The last licensee was Charles Victor Townsend. One man there as the last pints were drawn, was Johnny Ullmann, a director of Dover Demolition and Erection Company, who has pulled down more of the town's old public houses than he cares to remember. A new Salutation was built, but twenty yards further away from the Library. Behind the new buildings a large new telephone exchange was built soon afterwards.

48 Hundreds of local people will remember having a drink at The Cause is Altered public house, a former smugglers' haunt which stood at the top of Queen Street near St Mary's School, until planners decided it stood in the way of a new dual carriageway along York Street. Thankfully a campaign to prevent the road being bulldozed through the buried remains of Roman buildings succeeded, but hopes of saving the former Black Horse pub, as it was originally known, were dashed. Not even the historic 'plaque' recording that the ancient Cow Gate, in the old town wall, stood close by, appears to have been saved. Miller John Mannering, who, I believe, took this picture, thought the curious name of the pub derived from the fact that in the Civil War many in East Kent backed the Cromwellian cause. Then, on the landing of Charles II they pledged support for the monarchy and the name was changed. But historian John Bavington Jones, in 1906, said licensee Mr. Bourn in taking over the former smugglers' haunt at the beginning of the 19th century resolved to make a change for the better, and coined the new name.

49 This interesting old photograph is of the Mail Packet Inn which was in the St James Street area, later devastated by war. The postcard view is dated July 1907 and was shown to me by the late Sidney King, an avid collector of Old Dover memorabilia. The Mail Packet, with Stephen Markwick the licensee, was at 37 Woolcomber Street. He is probably the man in the doorway wearing slippers. Next door was William Slatter, a baker, whose premises were on the Woolcomber Lane corner. This lane connected Woolcomber Street with Trevanion Street which was nearer Castle Hill. On the opposite side of the lane was G. Hogbin the fishmonger. All the surviving properties in Trevanion Street, along with those on the Castle side of Woolcomber Street were demolished after the Second World War and the site is now occupied by the Dover Sports Centre and its car parks.

50 One of the largest public houses in the town was the Queen's Head Hotel in Biggin Street. Like the adjoining Salem Baptist Church, it was one of the town's distinctive landmarks until 1970 when it was demolished to build a bigger Boots the chemists. What a shame! Both should have been listed buildings and protected. The Baptist Church was built in 1840 by Dover brewer Alfred Kingsford at his own expense. It was enlarged in 1879 and in the early part of this century meeting rooms and a Sunday School were built at the rear with access from Edwards Road. The Boots plan saw the church move to Maison Dieu Road, near the junction with Ladywell. Completion of the new shop led to the closing of both Timothy Whites' and Boots' old stores, which stood on opposite corners of Worthington Street.

51 St Paul's Roman Catholic Church in Maison Dieu Road, faces the entrance to Pencester Road. It was built in the years 1867-68 and was the first permanent settlement of the Roman Catholics in the town, although there had been a Dover mission for years before that, from 1822. Mass was said in a variety of places, including a house in Snargate Street and a carpenter's loft in St James' Street. The first church seems to have been a converted Wesleyan chapel opened in 1835 in Elizabeth Square, now disappeared, the site of which is crossed by the Viaduct road link from Snargate Street to Lord Warden Square. St Paul's Church was built on the site of Johnson's nursery gardens, bought in 1864 for £450, and was officially opened in May 1868 by Archbishop Manning of Westminster and Dr. Grant, Bishop of Southwark. This photograph was taken a few years after the opening, when the surrounding land was being offered for sale for building purposes. The glass plate negative of this photograph still survives.

52 Still a landmark in Folkestone Road although twice devastated by enemy action in successive world wars but subsequently rebuilt, the Wesley Methodist Church, built in 1910, and adjoining Wesley Hall is no longer used by the Methodists, but has been taken over for use by Dover College. It is pictured here, with a porch, before its destruction by an enemy bomb on 24th September, 1917. Every one of the buildings opposite has disappeared, due to modern development, as have the trams, one of which, with open seats on top, is heading for Maxton. The church was left roofless after being hit by a 200lb bomb dropped by a German aircraft but, remarkably, the wooden chairs were left standing in neat rows. The opening of the church in November 1910 was marked by a tea party at the Salem Baptist Church hall, off Edwards Road, and a public meeting. One of the treasures to survive enemy attacks on Dover was the pulpit which had been used by celebrated preacher John Wesley when he spoke at the former Elisabeth Square Chapel (see postcard 56).

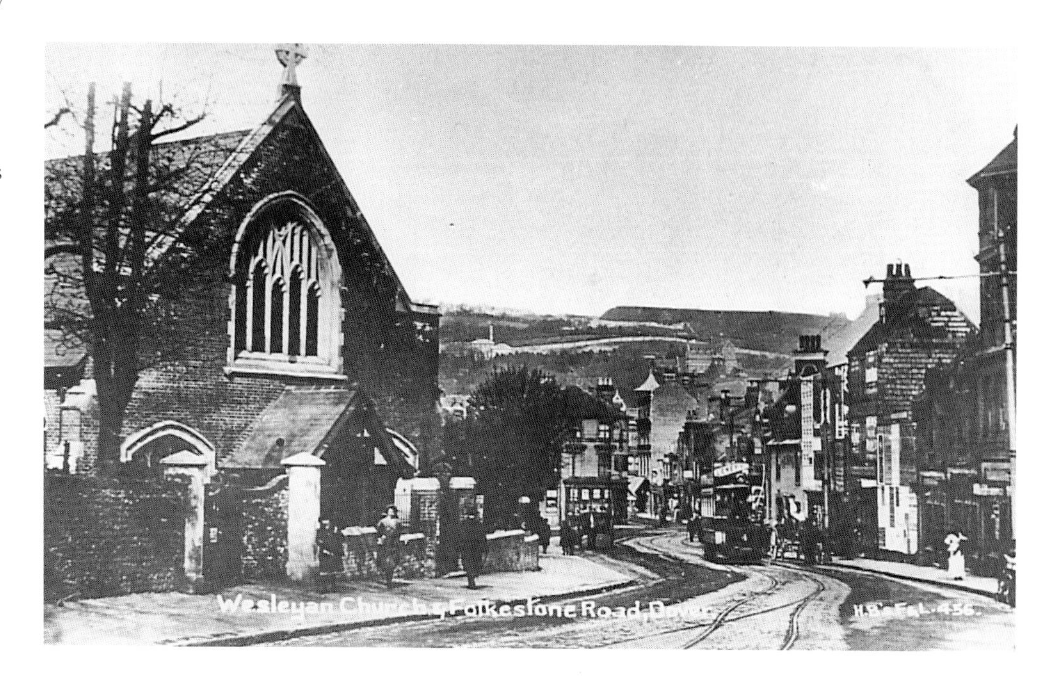

53 A little chapel steeped in history is St Edmund's in Priory Road, Dover. Bishop Richard of Chichester, after consecrating the chapel in 1253 AD, collapsed and died at mass in the Maison Dieu. He lay in state in the chapel a few days before burial in Chichester Cathedral. His viscera were buried in a casket before the high altar of St Edmund's. The Bishop had been in East Kent recruiting men to join the Crusades in the Holy Land. The chapel later fell into disuse. It was re-discovered when adjoining property in Biggin Street was being cleared for rebuilding in the 1760s, revealing human bones. In 1875 the floor of the adjoining Comet Inn collapsed, revealing coffins, and antiquarians realised it was St Edmund's Chapel. Over the next century the building was used as a blacksmith's or whitesmith's workshop, and a store. Between the two World Wars it became Isaacson & Mason's forge which features in a drawing by Mabel Martin, used as a postcard in 1939. Then Toc H charity workers used it to mend toys for needy children. This photograph was taken about 1965 when developers threatened to demolish it. Father Terence Tanner of St Paul's Roman Catholic Church led a battle to save it, and succeeded.

54 St Bartholomew's Church, consecrated in 1879, was built to serve the expanding Tower Hamlets housing estate. This postcard view dates from 1912. Declared redundant in comparatively recent times due to falling congregations, the church has been demolished and homes built on the site, at the corner of London Road and Templar Street. Before it had even opened there was major upset for the Church over one of the stained glass windows which depicted the Virgin Mary nursing the infant Jesus and men in adoration before her. The Bishop of Dover reported this to the Archbishop and his Grace promptly ordered the minister to remove it before consecration day and called for a sketch of any proposed new window to be shown to him before it was installed. The Dover Express newspaper did not seem surprised the minister had ignored the order, but expressed surprise there had been no objection to a life-sized sculptured image of Christ over the communion table which the congregation also bowed to on entering the church. A few weeks after the consecration the window was suppressed.

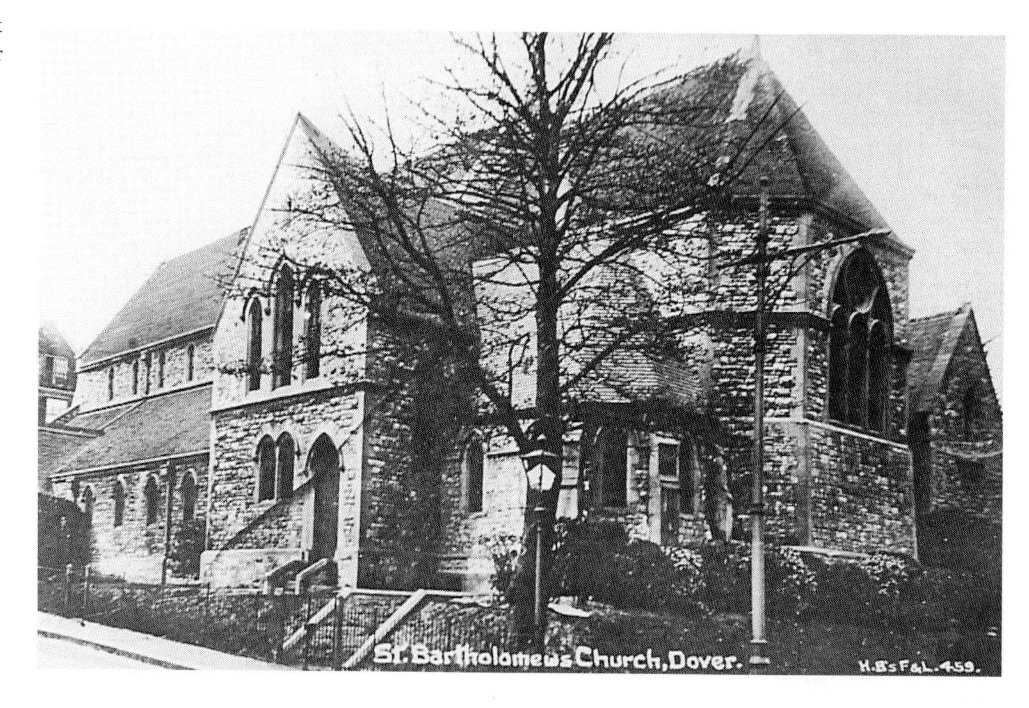

55 St Barnabas Church, sandwiched between Barton Road School and small shops in Cherry Tree Avenue, had a remarkably short life. Built in 1901-02 when church-going was having a revival, it subsequently became a victim of enemy action in the Second World War. It was very badly damaged, possibly due to its close proximity to the Dover gas works in Coombe Valley, which were a natural target. The foundation stone was laid by Mr. Robert Hesketh Jones J.P., on 9th October, 1901 and the church was built in stages. It opened the following year when there was still £3,000 to raise. But the first minister, the Reverend C.H. Golding-Bird was so popular, a growing congregation soon created the need for more space, and a corrugated iron annexe was put up on the site of what eventually became the nave. With depleted church membership, after the Second World War, St Barnabas, like the New St James' Church, in Maison Dieu Road, became redundant. St Barnabas was demolished in 1954.

56 June 3rd 1834 was a big day for the Wesleyans, pioneers of evangelical Christianity, when the foundation stone of the old Wesleyan Chapel in Snargate Street was laid. The chapel is pictured next to the entrance to the military Grand Shaft staircase to barracks above. The ornate entrance to this staircase has recently been rebuilt as part of an improvement scheme following the building of the new A20 road. This chapel was the Methodists' third in Dover, the first being in the old Pier district and the second at Buckland. The move to Snargate Street from the Pier was a sign of their growing congregations and the need for a bigger church. A thousand spectators were admitted to the site by tickets for the ceremony. Others looked down from the cliff-top. The chapel opened for services in October the same year and among treasured features was a pulpit from which John Wesley had preached about seventy years before. It was transferred from the Elizabeth Square chapel which had been made redundant by the new one. In 1934 a centenary sermon was preached from it. The chapel, which was demolished in 1965, incorporated a large hall.

57 Old St James' Church, as it was called after the building of New St James' Church in nearby Maison Dieu Road, is one of the town's older churches and has been preserved as a 'Tidy Ruin' following devastating war damage. The church was first hit by an enemy shell from across the Channel in 1942. Work began immediately to repair it but while this was being done another shell, again wide of its intended naval or military target, completed the devastation. The structure weakened, the tower eventually fell down and the building had to be made safe. This postcard picture, with a young family posing for their photograph against the churchyard wall, dates from the First World War when the church was in a newly restored condition. Preserved in Dover Museum is a Cinque Ports Court of Admiralty seat rescued from the church.

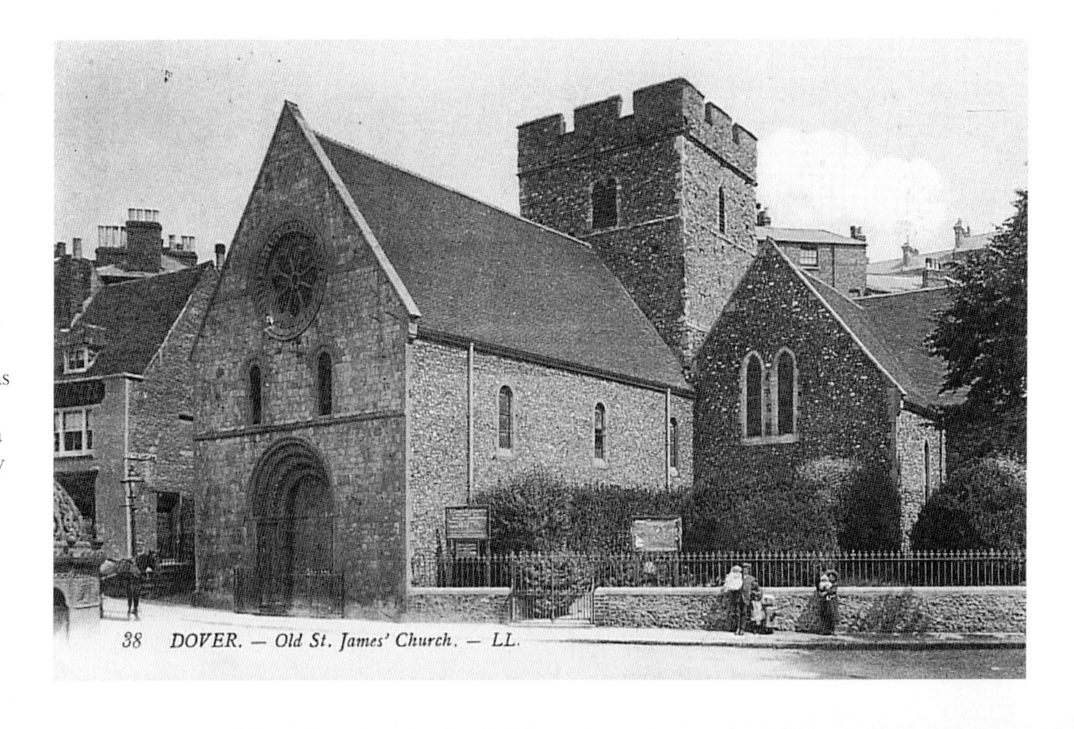

58 This interesting picture of St Mary's Church was taken from an unusual angle made possible by the demolition of a large block of buildings in Cannon Street (pictured on another page) just before the turn of the century, so the glass plate negative from which it is printed is a century old. This block of shops and flats extended from the footpath along the side of the churchyard to the Market Square. Boarded-up shop fronts opposite the church indicate more old properties on the other side of Cannon Street were about to be demolished for re-development. This was to build the Metropole Hotel and adjoining shops as pictured on another page. Beyond the church is the old Wellington public house, pulled down in recent times to build a supermarket which has now been converted into smaller shops.

59 Originally known as the Primitive Methodist Church, the London Road Methodist Church was built in 1901-02 on the old boundary between Dover and Buckland. The church had grown from a small mission, meeting above an old cow shed in nearby Brook Street in the late 1840s. The Primitive Methodists later built a chapel in Peter Street which was made redundant by the new church, which seems to have been a composite development, with a row of shops on the London Road frontage, while the church entrance was in Beaconsfield Road. The foundation stone was laid by the Mayor, Alderman W.J. Barnes JP. Two members, Mr. Charles Lewis and Mr. G. Brisley, were the builders. The church was damaged in the Second World War but subsequently restored and later a fine hall and meeting rooms were added. The shop on the left has Igglesden & Graves' name on the fascia.

60 Old St Mary's School, on the right, near the top of Queen Street was established as Dover Charity School, lower down the same street, on the opposite side of the road, in 1789. It is said to have been linked with Robert Udney's council school for six poor children set up in the old Court Hall, in the Guildhall in the Market Square, in 1616. The school pictured was built in 1820, not far from the old Zion Chapel (later a cinema) which is just visible across the entrance to Last Lane. This was called the Dover National School and a sign indicated it was 'Supported by voluntary contributions'. Intended to serve all the town it had space for 200 boys and 200 girls, while a separate building housed the infants. Special fund raising collections were held regularly at services in St Mary's and St James' churches, until government aid became available about 1862. When the time came to widen the adjoining York Street and turn it into a dual carriageway, St Mary's had to move to a new school built between Ashen Tree Lane and Laureston Place. The old school with an annexe building, next to The Cause is Altered public house, was then demolished.

61 Arguably Dover's most impressive looking school the Boys' Grammar School, for many years known as the County School, was built between 1929 and 1931, levelling of the site having begun much earlier in March 1924. It was built by J.J. Clayson of Lyminge, to replace the old school in Frith Road, which is now the Girls' Grammar School. Even earlier the school had been temporarily housed in Ladywell. Built on two terraces on the lower part of the Whinless Down with spacious playing fields the new school originally occupied 25 acres, part of which was given by an anonymous donor. Boys moved in at the beginning of the autumn term in 1931, the school being originally designed for 500 pupils. The official opening came later, when Prince George, later King George VI, drove a car to the site from Canterbury, on December 9th to perform the ceremony.

62 The ill-fated Castlemount School, for many years one of the town's Secondary Moderns, could truly be said to be a school with a history, and a ghost! The building dated back to 1879 when it was run as a high-class preparatory school for boys by Mr. Robert Chignell. Then in 1911 it was taken over by French monks known as Les Frères des Ecoles Chrétiennes who came to England because of an anti-clerical movement in France and established it as a training centre for teachers. It must be from this time that the ghost stories began. It is said the school was haunted by a ghost known as the Black Monk. In the First World War the school had a narrow escape from destruction. The monks had left and the military took over the building and were using it as barracks, when the very first bomb to hit Dover fell barely a metre from the perimeter wall. The monks returned after the war but eventually the school was taken over by Kent Education Committee and turned into the mixed secondary school we came to know so well. In June 1973 the main building was devastated by fire, believed to have been arson. A new Castlemount School was built but in recent years was closed.

63 Originally located in Chelsea where it was founded by Field Marshal Frederick, Duke of York (son of King George III) the Duke of York's Royal Military School moved to Dover in 1909. It was purpose-built to teach 'Sons of the brave', the school motto, in a more healthy atmosphere than the City. In 1921 the curriculum was modified on secondary school lines but the school carried on much as a boys' battalion, with the several boarding houses organised as military companies under pensioner warrant officers of the Regular Army. Then, from 1945 it was run very much as the Army's own public school, giving free education to sons of soldiers from the age of nine, with preference going to those whose brave fathers had died for their country or given long service. By 1953 numbers at the well-equipped school, of 170 acres, had risen to 426. It gradually became less military, but the annual passing-out parade at the end of summer term was one of the local events of the year. In recent years it has become a co-educational school.

64 The Gordon Boys Orphanage in St James' Street, Dover, was founded by Thomas Blackman in the mid-1880s to care for and educate orphans. It was a popular local institution which supplied recruits to more than sixty regiments in the British Army and to the Royal Navy, until the Second World War forced it to move to a safer district. In the first twenty years about 900 boys passed through the home. Some became farmers in Canada and Australia, others ended up in a variety of professions. An earlier seaside rest home was set up in nearby Liverpool Street in 1881 and in the fifth year cared for a thousand children. Mr. Blackman, who was born in Dover, where his mother ran a preparatory school, taught for fifteen years at Dover College. He decided the town needed an orphanage and set up a home in St James Street, naming it after General Gordon of Khartoum. The boys were all taught to fend for themselves, to swim and to take part in sports. They formed a band which created quite an impression at local events, all the boys being dressed in tartan. Mr. Blackman, a life member of the Dover and East Kent Scottish Society, received many awards for his work. He died in 1921, aged 74.

65 A solemn scene at the quayside of Dover's Admiralty Pier as the body of an unknown soldier is brought back from the battlefields of France on board the destroyer Verdun, some time after the First World War. Encased in an oak coffin draped with the Union Jack the soldier was one of many un-identified victims of the long, bloody conflict, but in death he was destined for considerable public adulation and glory. He was given a State funeral. His coffin was carried through the ranks of a hundred holders of the Victoria Cross and many VIPs on its way to burial in Westminster Abbey where a special tomb was built for him, the Unknown Warrior. By the end of Armistice Day 1920, the day of interment in the Abbey, 200,000 people had visited his graveside. He represented more than 300,000 British and Dominion soldiers with no known grave. Requests have recently been made for a plaque on the Admiralty Pier marking the place of the warrior's return to his homeland.

66 Few local events have created more public interest than the first aeroplane flight across the English Channel, by Frenchman Louis Bleriot on 25th July, 1909. Thousands of postcards, commemorating the event have been sold. A manufacturer of motor car headlamps, Bleriot won a coveted £1,000 prize, given by the Daily Mail, for the flight. Another pioneer, Herbert Latham, ditched in the sea in an attempt five days before. Bleriot, who had an injured foot, walked to his frail little craft with the aid of crutches, and took off at 4.37am. Guided by smoke from a French destroyer, he spotted St Marga-ret's Bay twenty minutes after leaving France. Turning towards Dover his aircraft was caught by the wind and he made a crash landing in Northfall Meadow, behind the Castle, breaking the undercarriage and propeller. Two French colleagues, Coastguardsman Richard Tems and other coastguard families were supposedly the only witnesses, but through the years many others have called at the Dover Express offices to claim the 'distinction'. Certainly a group of East Cliff boatmen, some soldiers and PC Standen were soon on the scene. Many more missed the landing because they were told he would land much further west.

67 Rolls-Royce partner, the Hon. Charles Rolls, at Dover on 2nd June 1910 preparing for his historic flight from Swingate, Dover to France and back without stopping. Rolls took off at 6.28am, circled the airfield opposite the Duke of York's School, climbed to about 800 feet and was soon lost to sight. Sighted on his return flight at 7.45 approaching the coast, he turned across the harbour, passing over the town at 1,000 ft to the sound of syrens and hooters. He circled the castle, crossed over the recently built Bleriot memorial, and landed close to his hangar at 8pm. Soldiers and police had to hold back a 3,000 strong crowd who had witnessed the event. After describing how he had dropped messages to the French over Sandgatte, he was hoisted shoulder-high by a cheering crowd and carried to his car. The flight, of about sixty miles, was done for the love of flying and it earned him the Ruinart Cup, said to be worth £90, given by the French. The Harbour Board tug Lady Curzon acted as a safety vessel. One month later the airman was dead, killed at a Bournemouth air show.

68 The scene at Swingate, behind Dover Castle, during the filming of The Conquest of the Air in 1935. This featured a reconstruction of the historic first balloon flight across the Channel in 1785 by Blanchard and Jeffries, using local extras. Filming created considerable excitement as thousands watched ballooning expert Dr. Dolfuss make a perfect ascent and drift over the town for nearly half an hour, before coming down in the sea off Shakespeare Beach. There, cameramen on the Dover tug Lady Duncannon took shots of it bouncing on the water and the occupants desperately throwing everything overboard, including their clothes, as in the original flight when the balloon came down low near Calais before landing successfully. They also recreated Bleriot's triumphant first crossing on his 'flying bicycle' as some witnesses dubbed his frail aircraft, in 1909, and the earlier ditching in the Channel of Samuel Latham's little aeroplane, the same year. More than 350 film extras were provided by Dover employment exchange and the Army found 300 soldiers to assist.

69 Half a dozen heavily laden Foden steam lorries were used to test the strength of a new Limekiln Street road bridge over the main railway line to Folkestone between Dover Priory Station and Beach Street, in 1923. The combined load was estimated at ninety tons. In the background is the now demolished Holy Trinity Church. The bridge formed a link between Snargate Street and Old Folkestone Road, with roads branching off to Lord Warden Square over the Viaduct on the seaward side, and to Archcliffe and the Western Heights on the inland side. Dover's MP, Major the Hon. J.J. Astor, opened the bridge saying it would improve access to the Marine Station, avoiding the congestion that used to occur at the old railway level crossing at Crosswall Quay. The same day the MP opened the Astor Avenue link between High Street and Elms Vale Road. This had provided work for the town's many unemployed and took the route of an old footpath called Fan Hedge. Major Astor could not have foreseen that the new A20 road, built in the early 1990s, would one day cut through from Folkestone to join up with a widened Snargate Street at this point.

70 Massive crowds lined Dover streets for this procession in 1914. The 155th Lord Warden of the Cinque Ports Earl Beauchamp and many distinguished visitors drove through the Market Square en route to the ancient Bredenstone, on the Western Heights overlooking the harbour, for the traditional Lord Warden's installation ceremony. Accompanied by the Countess and their son Viscount Elmley, the Earl, in the uniform of an admiral, had first joined a long procession of horse-drawn carriages to the Castle Keep for a meeting to appoint a new speaker of the Cinque Ports. Riders of the Royal East Kent Mounted Rifles, the local home guard, then formed an escort for the colourful procession down the hill, through Castle Street to Worthington Street and Military Road to the heights for the Court of Shepway ceremony at which the Earl was sworn into office to the accompaniment of a Lord Warden's salute of nineteen guns. Destroyers and other craft in the harbour were dressed overall for the occasion, and HMS St George provided a guard of honour at the Town Hall for a banquet which followed.

71 The run-down Hotel de France at New Bridge in July 1971 before demolition to make way for the dual-carriageway link between Townwall Street and the new widened York Street. Few people probably realise that the hotel was originally Batcheller's Library, built in 1826, once a great social centre. W. Batcheller was one of Dover's early authors and publishers, producing guide books and engravings of local scenes. Little altered in appearance, the old building was converted into a hotel in 1950, and the opening ceremony took place on 30th June which coincided with the arrival of a colourful cavalcade of veteran cars heading for a rally in France. The building had stood derelict for ten years. The hotel was built to accommodate some of the large number of tourists heading for the Continent on motor coach tours, which were becoming popular. The small square-paned windows facing New Bridge were those of the Café de Paris, one of the memorable features of the hotel.

72 The new Dover lifeboat Sir William Hillary takes to the water as the Duke of Windsor, then Prince of Wales and President of the RNLI, officially names the craft and launches her from the Wellington Dock slipway in January 1930. Nearly twice as fast as any other lifeboat the craft was named after the founder of the lifeboat institution. She was built following concern about the growing number of flying casualties in the Dover Strait, as passenger flights across the Channel increased. The Prince arrived by air, landing at the old Swingate aerodrome opposite the Duke of York's Royal Military School, as did the Under Secretary of State for Air and other officials. The Sir William Hillary was joined at the dock by a new Calais lifeboat and another fast new craft earmarked for the Shetlands. Fitted with two twelve-cylinder Thornycroft petrol engines each punching out 375 bhp, the new Dover boat had a speed in excess of seventeen knots. She was 64ft long, had a crew of seven and could carry in excess of one hundred people if required, but when war came the lifeboat station was closed down temporarily and the lifeboat sold to the Admiralty.

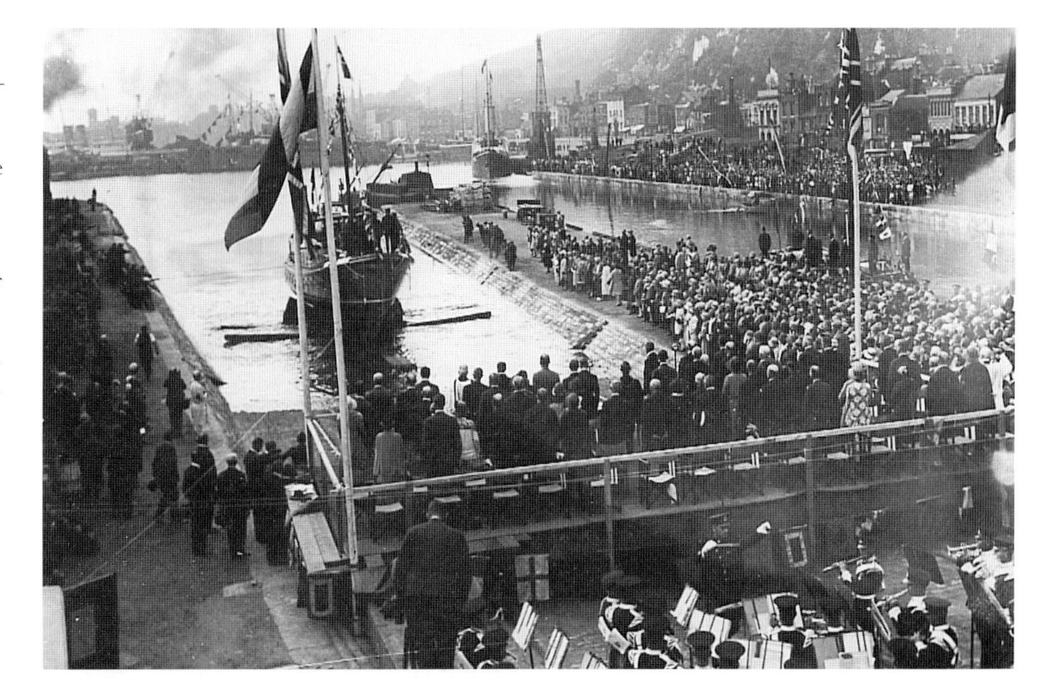

73 Over six feet in height, weighing more than 590 lbs (42 stone), and having a waist measurement of around 85 inches, Thomas Longley was for years 'the heaviest British subject in the world' according to this commemorative postcard. It is possible this card was one of those sold by Thomas Longley himself at his Church Street public house the Star Inn. A member of an old and respected Dover family, he was born in Snargate Street in 1848, the son of a butcher (thought to be William Longley) who was himself six feet tall. Because of his weight, Thomas Longley was a celebrity and was once offered £1,000 to go to America but declined. He died in 1904 aged 56 and his funeral created great public interest. The coffin was seven ft long and there were ten bearers at the funeral at St Mary's Cemetery, Copt Hill, with additional help needed to carry the remains up the slope. Thousands watched the procession and there was an estimated 2,000 to 3,000 at the graveside. There were wreaths from his widow and children, sisters and grandchildren. I was once shown his ring, which was about the size of a 50 pence piece in today's coinage.

74 One of the worst tragedies of the Second World War for Dover was the loss off the North Foreland, with all the crew of about sixty, of the Post Office Cable Ship Alert. This operated from a quay in the old Camber, now filled in and part of the Eastern Docks car ferry terminal. Ironically the ship was lost in 1945, within months of the end of the war. For fifty years the In Memorium columns of the Dover Express newspaper recalled that fateful day when the ship was believed to have been torpedoed by the enemy. At the time, presumably for security reasons, there was no official announcement. Since the war there have been several pleas from descendants of the crew for a memorial in a local church to the brave men.

75 One of Dover's most remarkable townsmen was Sir William Crundall who was mayor no less than thirteen times, a record never likely to be beaten. He followed his father onto the Town Council in 1883 and was first chosen mayor in 1886. He pressed for road widening in the congested town centre and helped persuade the council to open a badly needed public tramway service in the town in 1897. Also an important man behind the scenes in Dover was Mr. E. Worsfold Mowll, of the well-known family of lawyers with whom Sir William is pictured. The veteran 'Register' of Dover Harbour Board accompanied Sir William on a trip to see the Kaiser in 1901. Effectively chairman of Dover Harbour Board, Mr. Crundall's aim was to persuade the Germans to make Dover a port of call for the massive trans-Atlantic liners and when the first Hamburg-American liner had successfully berthed at the Prince of Wales Pier on 26th July 1903, the Kaiser sent a telegram congratulating Dover on the initiative. Born in Dover in 1847 William Crundall, who lived at Woodside, Kearsney, was a member of a local family of ship builders and timber merchants. He became a successful builder, developing the Barton Road and Castle Avenue areas. He found time to serve as a councillor and magistrate and was associated with Dover Harbour Board for 48 years. He became its chairman in 1906 and was still attending to its business when he died aged 86 in 1935.